Angels
of Whimsy

Angels of Whimsy

Everyday poems to inspire joy, laughter, and prayer

NANCY CORBETT

proving
press

Book Design & Production:
Columbus Publishing Lab
www.ColumbusPublishingLab.com

Copyright © 2020 by
Nancy Corbett
LCCN: 2020922399

Paperback ISBN: 978-1-63337-451-5
E-Book ISBN: 978-1-63337-452-2

Printed in the United States of America
1 3 5 7 9 10 8 6 4 2

INTRODUCTION

"Bless you."

Remember when your grandmother patted you on the head and spoke these words?

It's a pleasant memory, right? Well, that's my intention as I share my "angel poems" with you. It's my hope that these will be little rhymes and ponderings that cheer you, or make you think, or both. Each has an accompanying Bible verse to add a bit of credibility. Some ideas repeat, but ultimately one is interwoven throughout—that no matter who we are as to age, ethnic background, great in strength, or broken, God loves us!

"Hope—the angel by my mirror" came first. Kristi, at our local Christian book store gave her to me since she had only one wing. I laughingly asked Kristi if she thought I had a home for fallen angels, but later I looked around and saw *angels everywhere* in my house. Perhaps that's true of you too. My family and friends seemed to enjoy the poems that came along after Hope. My "primary" angels were the delicate glass figures in varying colors and postures, but a few secondary ones like "Snuffie" and "Mabel" made it into the group of my favorites.

You'll have to suspend reality a little if you have studied Biblical angel lore. Nevertheless, it's with a whimsical heart that I hope the book is a cheerful blessing to you.

Nancy Corbett

AMBER

She stands by the desk pen in my room.
I'm thinking of writing a letter.
My friends may need some word of cheer,
Hoping they're feeling better.

Perhaps it's a birthday they're having,
Or some other happy event.
Maybe I'm simply inquiring
How recent time has been spent.

Amber's skirt looks almost like sunlight.
She reflects rays into the room.
Her brilliant yellow is warming
Her wings seem to brush away gloom.

Of late, like Amber, I'm happy.
Christ is at work in my heart.
So sending a pleasant letter or card
Is simply doing <u>my</u> part.

Carry each others' burdens, and in this way you will fulfill the law of Christ.

Galations 6:2 NIV

BLANCHE

Blanche cannot be restrained by rhyme.
She is transparent in appearance...as well as in her
thinking.

She speaks: *Where I am positioned, I watch the back yard.*
Even in empty-branched winter, I <u>know</u> spring will
come again.
In my mind I foresee ...

Happy-faced maroon and yellow pansies, red geraniums,
orange begonias,
Purple lavender, pink and white sweet peas and dark green
yarrow-awaiting its blossoms
Thyme, basil, mint, rosemary, parsley, and more.

There's a dog box, seldom inhabited since the canine compo-
nent prefers in-house comfort.
A tall maple with numerous knotholes will become an apart-
ment complex bent on diversity
For grey, black, and brown squirrel families.

Birdfeeders will come back to life. Cardinals, Blue jays, a
crimson-headed Woodpecker,
Little dark Sparrows and other welcome visitors. Yellow
Finches will perch on their feeder again.

At times, three dogs will romp about—barking at squirrels,
deer …and the neighbors!
A sleek, striped cat will patrol the perimeter outside the fence;
but a stubby white cat
Will roll in the catnip inside the enclosure. She is too heavy to
pose a threat to the birds,
Who chirp in laughter at her antics.

4

How could anyone miss the lesson of the back yard—a kind of microcosm for
God's Magnificent creation!

Mankind still longs for Eden—aware that other angels guard its entrance now.
Meanwhile he loves the beauty of what is left and can say:
"IT IS GOOD."

There is a time for everything and a season for every activity under heaven.

Ecclesiastes 3:1

CHARITY...
A FISCAL DRAMA

Mortal: Your sparkling gown is a sight to behold.
You look quite regal with your wings of gold.
But I am puzzled by the item you hold.

Charity : It's an abacus.

Mortal: An abacus—Just what is an abacus?
        Is it the father of Scout in *To Kill a*

Mockingbird? Abacus Finch?
Is it a bus filled with bad-talking people,
going to an abbey...Abbey-cuss?
Sounds like a book of the Bible...Please
turn to Abacus 2:9.

Charity: It's none of those. It's the fourth word in the
Oxford American Dictionary,
  right after "a-back." In fact, dear Mortal,
  you might be taken aback
  to learn that an abacus is "a frame
  containing parallel rods with beads
  that slide up and down for <u>counting</u>."
I'm holding one here, beside this giant piggy
bank because I'm your reminder about
Money!

Mortal: Money?

Charity: Remember the widow's mite: two small coins,
but it was ALL she had.
  Jesus praised her generosity.

How about the rich young ruler, who valued
his wealth over following Jesus?
Where do you stand in this, Mortal?
>Must I slip into your pocketbook and
>help you open your wallet
>when the plate goes by? Should I
>position myself with your checkbook
>or with your credit cards?...nodding when
>you have given enough?

I'm reminding you—and the truth may smart.
God only requires that you do your part.
Where your treasure is—<u>there</u> will be
your heart!

*Give and it will be given to you, a good measure—
pressed down, shaken together and running over—
will be poured into your lap. For with the measure
you use, it will be measured to you.*

Luke 6:28

I SPEAK TO...
COLLEEN

Thoughts of Ireland fill my head.
My dreams play out in green.
I'd like to go there once again.
Retirement check's too lean!

I look at films and read the books
And think of soda breads,

Plus shamrocks and small leprechauns,
Green fields, like quilted spreads.

The banshees shriek sometimes at night.
They keep me from my sleep.
If I could get to Ireland,
I could just count Irish sheep

Is it bad to wish or dream?
I hardly think it so.
Do you think I'm whining far too much.
Should I just let it go?

My family's great; I love my home,
My church, my work, my friends.
I'm thankful for so very much.
The list just never ends.

What do you think, Irish angel?

Sit down, American Lady.
You feel your roots are strong.
I'll sing a verse of "Danny Boy"
And you can sing along.

I know you have some Waterford.
Fill a glass with Irish brew.
Bad idea…don't do that!
I didn't say that to you.

There's no need to drown your sorrow
Or go to a local pub.
Stop whining; be glad for your blessings.
Put some Irish Spring in the tub.

Sure and Begorah, you've got all you need.
And this is my final thought:
Let go of yearning for what you don't have.
Be contented with what you've got!!!

Godliness with contentment is great gain.
                              I Tim 6:6

DAISY

She stands by the verse on the counter.
That's strength and dignity she's wearing.
She laughs at the future without fear.
A good message she is sharing.

She was to have watched the calendar.
Maybe she does, in a way;

Since she isn't afraid of the future
And trusts God day after day.

We all should be laughing as she does.
But don't you think it odd?
We often fear the days to come
When each is a gift from God.

•••••••••••

Remember the days of childhood
When we pulled petals one by one
To see if somebody loved us?
But that was just in fun.

"He loves me—he loves me not—"
Went the chant in our youthful voices.
Wouldn't that be a strange way
To make important choices?

We people of faith need not puzzle
Over whether God loves us or not.
If petals reflected the Bible,
I believe we have been taught:

He loves me.
   He loves me.
      He loves me.
         He loves me.

Cast all your anxiety on him because he cares for you.

I Peter 5:7

FAITH

Faith is clear about her job
Beneath the TV screen.
She listens as we watch it
And considers what we've seen.

Some days the shows are hopeful.
Most days the news is sad.
Sometimes it writhes with conflict.
It seems we've all gone mad.

Shootings, drugs, and murders,
Bombs, bigotry, wide-spread starvation,
Poverty, perversion...the question comes:
What's happened to our nation?

The mood is dark. The newsmen scream:
"Mankind is just depraved."
Behind the screen, there's a wide, wild world
That's waiting to be saved.

God will do that when men ask.
Each person has a choice.
And for each one who comes to Christ,
The angels all rejoice.

...including Faith

...I tell you, there is rejoicing in the presence of
the angels of God over one sinner who repents.
Luke 15:10

GIMPY

I first heard the name "Gimpy" during my col-
lege days when our "trio," my two roommates
and I, were required to sing as a Christian
Service Assignment in a Sunday night service
at God's Little Light House Mission in the
Bowery section of New York City. We were
accompanied by several ministerial students
who preached and led the singing.

It was a real eye-opener for this young college freshman, sitting on the platform, looking at folks who had lost their way. These men had to attend the service in order to share the meal provided afterwards and to spend the cold night inside. We were invited to eat at the mission staff table. It was then we met the mission mascot, their crippled cat Gimpy, beloved by everyone.

Over fifty years later I still recall the epiphany of realizing that these men, in spite of their being unshaven and disheveled, had not lost their basic humanity; they still felt caring affection for Gimpy who limped from table to table, the happy recipient of kind words and caresses. Perhaps these homeless men identified with the rough, scabbed, striped cat. He had once been a street fighter, but now had found safety and a new life with loving friends at God's Little Light House Mission.

GIMPY, THE GARDENER ANGEL

Now, I have a little garden figure I've named "Gimpy." She is disabled, having lost her leg and her shoe with a turned-up toe. It only seemed logical to equip her with a Q-tip leg replacement and bandage wrap to keep it in place.

She still works as a diligent "Gardener Angel." She oversees my houseplants! She has a winning smile and a ready watering can. Her dragonfly wings and regal crown add a touch of whimsy to her angelic aura. In her cream and yellow gown, she well may flit about among the plants unhampered by her "disability" when it's dark and quiet in the house. Her plants are doing quite well.

She has decided … when it is hard to walk, one learns to fly!

"But they that wait upon the Lord shall renew their strength; they shall mount up with wings as eagles; they shall run, and not be weary; and they shall walk, and not faint."

Isaiah 40: 31

GRACIE LOU

Gracie Lou, just who are you? ...

See that bar you hold in your hand?
Is it a bar for prying?
Were you there at the tomb
Where Jesus lay after dying?

Did you assist in rolling the stone
Away from the sepulcher door?

As the ground shook, and light flashed.
This event never happened before!

God could have moved the stone Himself,
But I like to think you were thrilled
To be a part of this miracle
As prophecies were fulfilled.

Did you announce that Jesus had risen
To the ladies awash with their grief?
Were you the one who shared the news
To their open-mouthed disbelief.

"HE IS NOT HERE; HE IS RISEN FROM
THE GRAVE! HALLELUJAH!"

Done with stone moving, your role had
changed.
The pry-bar became a baton.
Like a majorette, you led the group
For now a parade is on.

Tell the others that Jesus lives
And can live in our hearts as well.

What a great message, Gracie Lou,
You've been given the task to tell!

*And the angel answered and said unto the
women, Fear not; for I know that you seek Jesus,
who was crucified. He is not here: for he is risen
as he said.*

Matthew 28:5

HOPE
(ANGEL BY MY MIRROR)

My broken-winged angel
with halo on top
wasn't prepared for her
wing-wrenching drop.

She stands by my mirror
with only one wing.

I could, of course, glue her;
But...then...that's the thing...

Seeing her malady,
a message unspoken,
reminds me that
I, too, am broken

Only God's glue can
fix all my ills,
to keep me protected
from life's coming spills.

•••••••••••

Hold me together, God.
not just a wing.
Take all my brokenness;
Mend everything.

Therefore, if any man be in Christ, he is a new creature: Old things are passed away; behold all things are become new.

II Corinthians 5:17 KJV

MABEL

Mabel, the mobile angel,
 Observes from the kitchen curtain.
She used to be a lapel pin,
Whose origin is uncertain.

She must be amused by the woman,
Who fusses and fumes at the sink.
"What shall we have for dinner?"
Is all that **she** seems to think.

"Surely there's more in life than food.
Is what ___Mabel___ wants to say.
"Why don't you plant some flowers?
Or do something else today?"

"Of course, we know I'm an angel
So I'm sort of out of the loop.
But consider grilled cheese or pizza
And there's always tomato soup!

"'Sink-lady,' stop all of your stressing.
Reframe your thoughts for relief.
This is the day the Lord has made.
Isn't that still your belief?"

"Rejoice and be glad!   God's in control,
Even when days are unnerving.
And I'll be content when I see you smile
As I do my job of observing."

Do not be anxious about anything, but in
everything, by prayer and petition, with
thanksgiving, present your requests to God.
Phillippians 4:6

PERIWINKLE

Periwinkle works on the kitchen sill.
She is no longer flying.
Only one wing is on her back.
She is not even trying.

She'd go in circles if she went airborne.
What a fix she would be in!
The other angels would cover their mouths
To stifle a growing grin.

She doesn't mind if they might smirk.
Being an example is part of her work.
She simply remembers that she is divine
And laughs at the spinning antics of mine.

Sometimes we all go in circles
And, while Peri's skirt is <u>blue</u>,
She **chooses** to be **happy**…
So I will do that too!

*May the righteous be glad and rejoice before
God; may they be happy and joyful.*
                    Psalm 68:3

RUBY

Ruby's reflected in the mirror
As she stands on the clock on the dresser.
She pretends my "jewels" are valuable,
But please don't really press her.

Down deep she knows my earrings
Were mostly just thrift shop finds.
She shakes her head at the number
And colors and shapes of all kinds.

You have only two ears, dear lady.
And what about watches and pins?
Be aware that loving possessions
Is how gluttony begins!

What's really important here, instead
Is the clock on which I'm sitting.
It's TIME that is precious; it's very clear
Beyond what you've been admitting.

You simply glance at the time in passing.
You think you have plenty of it.
But if you only knew life's length.
You couldn't help but love it.

Daytime passes oh, so quickly.
Wasting time, you cannot afford.
Praise God for the time you have on earth
And use it to serve the Lord.

That doesn't mean to be frenzied.
The pace can be sure and steady.
But when the time comes to live your faith,
You simply need to be ready.

You'll probably work in the daytime
Or have other chores to complete.
That's the trouble with "daily-ness,"
It tends to repeat—repeat.

At night the "Ruby Reflected"
Takes over watching the clock.
You may be awake and worried
Or simply be taking stock.

"Let not your heart be troubled,"
Jesus said. That's what we're to do.
Remember every day, every hour,
Every minute, every second
God is loving and caring for you.

Come unto me, all ye who labor and are heavy
laden, and I will give you rest.

Matt 11:28

SNUFFIE

Snuffie, Snuffie—out of work!
Have you now retired?
My candles run on batteries;
A snuffer's not required.

Let's consider other skills
You may have. What are they?
Shelf-sitting is just not enough
To earn yourself some pay.

I see you have a trumpet.
Could you, maybe, join a band?
Having an angel in the group—
Some folks would think that grand.

Why not audition here and now?
Please play a number for us.
But, wait, perhaps you'd rather sing.
Were you in an angel chorus?

I recall you were a Christmas gift
And with your gown and wings,
You look as if you used to work
At special "hearaldings."

I know what it's like to age and think
Your value has diminished.
No one may need you anymore.
Perhaps your work life's finished?

But let's take heart, dear Snuffie.
This may be cause for cheering.
We still have talents yet to share…
There's always volunteering!

The righteous will flourish like a palm tree;
they will grow like a cedar of Lebanon, planted
in the house of the Lord, they will flourish in
the courts of our God.

*They will still bear fruit in old age, they will
stay fresh and green, proclaiming, "The Lord is
upright; he is my Rock, and there is no wicked-
ness in him."*

Psalm 92: 12-15

VIOLET

With no wings at all
Violet looks so small
But her spirit is still strong.
She's an angel in training
But is constantly straining
And hopes to earn wings before long.

She's dwarfed by the light
Where I read each night…
Devotional books and such.
She dotes on the Bible
And thinks God is liable
To grant wings that she wants so much.

But her hopes are sinking
For she's begun thinking:
"I'm just not up to snuff."
She has missed the part
About what's in her heart.
What she _does_ may not be enough.

With humans the reward
Comes from knowing the Lord,
Accepting His marvelous grace!
But angels, Violet, I understand,
Do their tasks at God's command.
You just have to keep the pace.

No need to _earn;_ just simply obey,
Serving God faithfully every day.
For both of us that's a good plan.
For the rest of our days
Let's give God praise
For his goodness to angels and man!

My grace is sufficient for you, for my power is made perfect in weakness.

II Cor 12:9

NUNS OF THE ABOVE
AN OVERVIEW

Sitting on my coffee table is a lovely white candle ring, brushed with gold. It appears to be six angels holding hands as they circle a candle. To me, they also look like nuns in their habits. I can't miss the symbolism that they join with other believers, like us, who want to spread the light of the Gospel throughout the world.

I found my old dog-eared copy of *Butler's Lives of the Saints* and looked for women saints who had been nuns. I thought it was a clever title, "Nuns of the Above," but in no way meant to be flippant in telling about them. My choices are arranged chronologically and note women from a number of countries and origins. I think this is another reminder that what is really important is our willingness and enthusiasm to serve, not necessarily our circumstances.

You may wish to join them in sharing the Light of the World with friends and family in your circle of life.

"Let your light shine before others, that they may see your good deeds and glorify your father in heaven."

Matthew 5:16

SAINT MONICA
(332-387)

Monica's child was a hellion.
Still she prayed and prayed and prayed
For her smart, young son's conversion;
But for years he could not be swayed.

When he moved from their home, she
followed
And she prayed and prayed and prayed.
A bishop called her foolish
For all the effort she made.

At last the son was converted,
A deep commitment was made.
Saint Augustine was very grateful
For a mother who prayed and prayed.

*The effectual fervent prayer of a righteous
(wo) man availeth much.*

James 5:18b

KATHERINE DREXEL
(1858-1955)

Katherine Drexler, possessions-blessed
With poor and needy was quite distressed.

She asked the Pope to send some help.
Recognizing the promise of this young whelp,

He asked her, being quite the visionary,
"Why don't YOU become a missionary?"

She took the challenge; many angers she faced.
Native Americans and Blacks she embraced.

Sisters of the Blessed Sacrament came from
her wealth
At seventy-six, she lost her health,

Committed to praying, 'til age ninety-seven
When she passed from this life into heaven.

Anyone who belongs to Christ has become a new person. The old life is gone; a new life has begun.
II Corinthians 5:17 NLT

THERESE OF LISIEUX
(1873-1897)

Born to a watchmaker's family,
Time was of the essence in
Therese's life.

Only 24 at the **time** of her death,
She had written *The Story of a Soul*
While in a cloistered convent in France.

It told of the way she spent her **time**,
Calling it "The Little Way."
Always being aware of God's presence.

Feeling insignificant, like a little flower,
She didn't have **time** to find prayers to recite,
But became a perpetual prayer herself.

When the **time** came for her to die
(Tuberculosis took its toll)
She did that with great courage and acceptance.

Let us take **time** to learn from her devoted youthful example.

To everything there is a season, and a time to every purpose under heaven.

Ecclesiastes 3:1

EDITH STEIN
(1891-1942)

Edith, born a Jew, searched for "the truth"
And found it when visiting a friend
Where she studied Teresa of Avila
Through writings Teresa had penned.

Meanwhile, Edith earned a doctorate
And continued her search for truth.
To calm her Orthodox mother,
She worshipped as in days of her youth.

Joining the Carmelite nuns in Cologne,
With tradition her name was changed,
Becoming Benedicta of the Cross.
But the German head was deranged.

She tried to escape The Holocaust,
But Hitler's reach was vast:
Sent to the Auschwitz death camp.
After suffering...she died at last.

"I have come as a light to shine in this dark world, so that all who put their trust in me will no longer remain in the dark."

John 12:46

MOTHER TERESA
(1910-1997)

How could a mere verse contain the essence of
this Nobel Prize-winning nun!

She lived in my time and became a significant
example for Christians and non-Christians
alike.   Over the years, I have read books and
articles about her work. There have been tele-
vision documentaries and coffee table picture
books showing her in her white cotton sari
with a blue border ministering to the poor and
dying in India. She lived her faith!

Born Agnes Bojaxhui in Serbia in 1910, she
served as a nun in a number of capacities but
eventually ended up in India. At that time in
her life, many religious orders had left India;
but she chose to stay and serve until, suffering
from exhaustion, she needed to go on retreat
for a month. It was on the train on her way
to retreat that she felt a supernatural call to

work with India's most poor. She founded the Missionaries of Charity.

Far from "retreating," she "advanced" the message that all of us should help needy brothers and sisters, be it in health or poverty. She urged individuals to serve in whatever way they are able, where ever they are. In the faces of all those for whom she cared, she saw Christ.

Naked? Hungry? Sick? Discouraged?...and the list goes on. This Saint Teresa of Calcutta believed and lived the Biblical admonition:

Inasmuch as you have done it unto one of the least of these, my brethren, you have done it unto me.

Matthew 25:40b KJV

SISTER MATILDA
(1919–2016)

This spirited Dominican nun came to my hometown to serve as a chaplain at Good Samaritan Medical Center, run by the Franciscan Sisters of Christian Charity. She was eventually one of the clergy participating in my wedding in 1984; she had become a dear friend.

She taught me, concerning hospital visitation, that it was important to touch the sick and dying; it was imperative that we move to a spot near the head of the bed to be easily seen and heard, rather than cowering at the end of the bed as if we too might be caught by "Death." She talked me into participating in a special quarterly service organized by her department to commemorate the lives of people who had died at the medical center during that period. What a beautiful time for families and friends to affirm the value of their loved ones' lives!

Some of her co-workers or patient families found her to be a bit too blunt, but I found her to be full of truth and light. One Sunday evening I attended a charismatic mass with her. Another worshipper seemed extra lively, supposedly speaking in tongues, but I was puzzled and asked Sister Matilda, "Do you think she is really speaking in tongues or is she just trying to gain attention for herself?"

There was a thoughtful pause. ... Sister Matilda responded, "I just have to leave that up to God." I was zapped!! Some time later, I reminded her of that moment and she told me she didn't even remember. But I did. In fact, I lovingly remember this special nun who mixed her deep devotion to her faith with practical everyday wisdom.

Retiring to the Mother House at St. Mary's of the Springs in Columbus, Ohio, she has now become a "Nun of the Above."

Now that I am old and gray, do not abandon me, O God. Let me proclaim your power to this new generation, your mighty miracles to all who come after me.

Psalm 71: 18

IN CLOSING

THE MORNING
AFTER
CHRISTMAS

Angels are playing patty-cake
Upon my windowsill.
When I went to bed last night
Everything was still.

They had clustered round
The manger scene, a holiday display.
Now they faced each other
And seemed to be at play.

My family did the dishes
After we'd all gorged ourselves.
They even put the stuff away
In fridge, and drawers, and shelves.

Not having kitchen duty,
I was thankful for their cleaning.
Meanwhile the spot above the sink
Spoke to all the Christmas meaning:

HAPPY BIRTHDAY, JESUS!

Someone in the family must
 Have changed the group a bit.
They knew I'd smile when I got up
And appreciate their wit.

But…

I found the playing angels
A lovely scene to view—
I wondered if the real ones
Had played with Jesus too.

AFTERWORD

The poems, stories, and biographies in this book were spontaneously joyful to write! Hopefully you found favorites and returned to some pages to re-read. The goal was to bless you and at last to remind you…

"He shall give his angels charge over you, to keep you in all your ways."

                                        Psalm 91:11

ABOUT THE AUTHOR

Nancy Corbett is a life-long resident of Zanesville, a small town in Southeastern Ohio. She earned her Bachelors of Arts in English at Nyack College in Nyack, New York; her Masters in Interpersonal Communication from Ohio University. With a variety of job experiences, including hospital public relations director, radio station "stringer," tv weather girl and children's show host, she discovered --at last-- that her true calling was teaching. She worked for thirty-nine years at Philo High School; then after retirement, she taught for ten more years as an adjunct instructor in communications at Zane State College but now has re-retired.

She is married to Bob, and in their blended family there are six adult children. Presently as an active member of Trinity Evangelical Lutheran Church in Zanesville, she feels she is a contented follower of the Good Shepherd and is waiting with enthusiasm to learn what new opportunities will be available now that she is "out to pasture."

CPSIA information can be obtained
at www.ICGtesting.com
Printed in the USA
LVHW020928110221
678898LV00010B/979

9 781633 374515